THE YEAR WEARS ITS SEASONS

Margaret Tynes Fairley

BAMBAZ Press

Los Angeles 2018

Acknowledgments

Mary Baldwin College Bulletin, Alumnae News Letter, Vol. XIX, November, 1948, No. 7, "Direction"

Mary Baldwin College Bulletin, Alumnae News Letter, Vol. XIX, November, 1948, No. 7, "Peony for Ann Going on Sixteen"

Mary Baldwin College Bulletin, Alumnae News Letter, Vol. XIX, November, 1948, No. 7, "The Published Year: To the Children of Green Acres School"

Miami Daily News, Florida Poets and Poets Visiting Florida: Anthology of Poems, 1940, "Pioneer Mother"

Miami Daily News, Florida Poets and Poets Visiting Florida: Anthology of Poems, 1940, "To the Strongest

Nature Magazine, May, 1938, "Wading in the Pool"

Radcliffe Poetry Club, *Radcliffe Poetry Anthology,* 1931, "Faith"

Silver Spring Post, May 29, 1940, "May"

Staunton News Leader, 1930's, "The Room"

The Yale Review, Autumn 1938, "Shadow and Light"

Cover Art: Baz Here
Book Design by Baz Here
Edited by Bambi Here

ISBN: 978-1978372207

Bambaz Press
548 S Spring Street
Suite 1201
Los Angeles, CA 90013
contact: Bambi@bambazpress.com

For Finley

Contents

Foreword
Editor: Bambi Here

Philip Booth, the novelist, said, "Writing poems is not a career but a lifetime of looking into, and listening to, how words see."

When Margaret Tynes Fairley's sons, William and James Fairley, asked me to read Margaret's work, it was a blow-back-hair experience. I began to read the 200-something poems I had in my inbox, handpicked by the family, from her boxes upon boxes of some typed, and some handwritten poems. And so began the journey.

As a mother and a poet myself, I know what it is to sneak out in the evening, under a street lamp, and hide in my car, parked in the driveway, with my feet hanging out the window, avoiding my screaming children, "No, I don't want a bath." Please let their dad help, just this one night, because I am busy here in the dark birthing a poem on the steering wheel.

As an editor, I understand how to gentle (and nudge) an artist's heart and I always promise to hold their work with my own bare hands. But this time, I was not able to work directly with the poet—Margaret died in 1986. Her sons are in their 70s and 80s. A legacy was in my hands now. I had to find a new way to learn how her "words see."

On the first read-through, I fell in love with her work. I imagined Margaret out in the garden in the 1920s, seeing the blooming of things in the middle of winter: "Zinnias are frozen brilliance" ("Last Signatures"). Or maybe she just sneaked a smoke.

You, dear reader, have the good fortune to experience a master poet: she who tucks metaphors into the emotional chaos of nature, uncovers our tender connection with an illusory world, rendering her words into seasons of sea, flowers, birds, and trees. I believe Margaret Tynes Fairley is one of the most accomplished poets of the 20th Century – as yet an "undiscovered" writer to a wider audience – but she should hold the place of a historic poet in the 1920s and 1930s, shaping metaphors and images into an enduring substance.

The Year Wears Its Seasons is a testament to her genius—with her scrupulous eye on sudden beauty, Fairley conceives our weary world with a celebratory song of joy announcing: "No audience but rock and air / And cattle grazing on the hills— / Yet still from every wind-arched leaf, / The cataract of music spills." ("Vermont Fall"). And in the opening poem of her book: "Dress me in motley / Let me play the fool. / The year wears its seasons / Was earth ever dull?" (Dress Me in Motley").

Skillful and elegant, she also explores themes of loss and redemption: "Will time beat down the blossom / Under a ghostly rain / And leave no seed to nourish / The frozen ground again?" ("The Question"). Deftly carving lines of acceptance: "Beneath our brows these stanzas / Are graven deep as bone / To carve the sterner skeleton / When fickle flesh is gone. / Above our heads these sentences / Are trumpet vines of joy / That climb the sunlit trellises / No winds may once destroy." ("The Poet").

With an interior worship and an outward gaze, Fairley says: "You brought me hyacinths / White as April snow / Ah, more, you brought the stem / Of spring itself. Ah, did you know / Now out of the darkness climbs the spirit / Slowly to the light again?" ("Hyacinths").

Margaret Tynes Fairley did not flinch. She knelt down in ever-bearing fields, whispered code to a body of roots and stars, and listened to how words see.

Dress Me in Motley

Dress me in motley
Let me play the fool.
The year wears its seasons
Was earth ever dull?

Not for the honor
Not for the gold
But for the love
Of crocus or cold.

Let me go wind wide
Over the trees,
Wear every season
And live as I please.

Dress me in motley
Green cap and bells.
Life but a somersault
Motion that tells—

Not for the duty
Not for the praise
But for the wonder
Of unhooked days.

Let me go dancing
In every court,
With mirth for each tumble
And bells for each hurt.

Acceptance of a Deeper Spring

—to my sons

Now that berries blood the dogwood tree
And spring invisible in pod
Contracts the volume of the year
To seed that stores a memory of green,
I can reverse my rush to bloom as well.
Only, the seed I now can store away
Will blossom in new hearts and harvest come
When I am one with memory and repeat
The life my death will nurture, for I know
The cyclic beauty of the dogwood flower
Throbs in a pulse remembering all
From that still fulcrum, mind, projection's power,
No matter what I see or do not see.
There is a deeper spring that only needs
The soul's apparel and the blood's
Acceptance of renewal on extended bough.

Poem

Only the lilacs hold the rain
In purple wells,
The trees must let it go
And leaves like bells
Ring drop on silver drop.

March and the Lamb in Virginia

Briar bright and big with bluff
Windy tight from swollen stuff
Of cloud and bud and dash of gold
Where crocuses corrupt the cold.

Large as hills relieved of snow
Tossing oak and making glow
Embers of the furrowed field—
What a month, a time to yield
The innocent, the trusting one.

Atom mite his day begun
In the teeth of breaking weather,
March and Lamb, the two together
Make the hardy stuff of spring,
Tustle, growth, and all she'll bring.

Virginia Spring

Redbud knots the mountainside
The cone-shaped hills are green.
Dogwood planes divide the light,
Where the leaf dark mold has been.

On forest floors, arbutus creeps
And tender bluet flower.
Lovers words are fragrant now
To snare this fleeting hour.

April and White Dogwood

April and white dogwood
Floats her discs of bloom
In the half-bare wood.
Floats the trees apart before
Summer freezes them in green
Under a sky of blue and gold and white.
There is one perfect moment in the year
When dogwood, winged as light and white as snow,
Angles all the woods
With some reflected ecstasy harboring in mind.
Then I know a clarity of joy distilled from all the months,
As dew condenses on the grass from heavy skies.

Tell him, winged perfection, let him find
All agonies are rites we practice while half-bound.
Freedom is limitation and discovery, reciprocal, within, without
The toil of years is often ours for this one glimpse of snow
Floating the woods apart, dimensioned on an April bough.

Hyacinths

You brought me hyacinths
White as April snow,
Belling sweetness on their emerald stems,
Fresh as water but so low
To earth it seems
They cling to warmth and darkness there
Before they break in whiteness on the air.

You brought me hyacinths
White as April snow.
Ah, more, you brought the stem
Of spring itself. Ah, did you know
Now out of darkness climbs the spirit
Slowly to the light again?
You must, for in your gift I found
Earth's old sorrow, April's stem of rain
Cupped in sweetness, white and emerald green.

Apple Tree

This web of bough on loom of sky,
This motion pattern, bud and leaf,
And color, rose, like heart of shell,
With scent of sun, of rain and spice
Bubbling from the bee bent flower;
This snow in April, tossed in light,
Spangled shadow, leaf and stem,
Against blue sky, up-wash of cloud,
Oh, what a tangled problem it would be
Except for this—
The all, together, floats an apple tree.

How Fair the Morning: Spring at Sausalito, California

How fair the morning in her lineaments of light.
The song of bird comes effortless as noon,
The hills are comforted by curve,
Serenely lie
Anchored yet free to test the sky.
A wind so gentle generation seems
No single point but all direction borne
Winks in the bay and glosses every pine.
How fair a haven for the griefs of man
This world he holds in carelessness or pride,
Wearing her beauty like a necklace for each mood
Or struggling for her secrets, every stride
Forward as difficult as birth and death.
Still, still she holds him, prods him,
Grants him such a day as this,
Each hour relaxed in time
And birdsong tender with delight.

To the Strongest

Eyes that meet and may not sunder
Hands that take the hearts sweet plunder
Down some lane where blossoms fountain
Underneath the moon's old mountain.

These shall know the red wing fleeting
April's bud and June's gold greeting,
These shall lie where snowdrops linger
Trace the leaf with love's warm finger.

Where the leveled hay lies longest
These shall reap and bind the strongest,
Find the crimson cockle flower
Cast aside by careless mower.

May

This is the month of the green leaf over
The empty bowl of the sky and the hollow
Space that was winter.
Lightly the oval leaf of the beech
Crowns the mild morning,
While the green spurs of male oak glitter,
Glitter from limbs once bare as the cold.
Now are the twisted boughs of the apple
Healed with a cloud, a tangle
Of green that falls to dapple
The ground beneath.

This is the month of life's abundance
Published at point of every twig,
Speech returning and song's abundance
Filling the meadows of air again.
Voice of the single leaf, of all summer,
Silvering, greening the earth again.

Green Roof

Now is the world roofed over with leaf
Palm to palm on the sky and the brief
Wild hour of strawberry spreads
In tents of green on the meadow beds.
Over, under, and all around
Whisper of green and shelter sound—
Full wide skirt of spring grown tall,
Upward each leaf and the shadow's fall.
O heart be calm as the growing tree.
Change is the stem of maturity
and this the roof that is wide and free.

Blown Bubble Clear

Hills and sea are cut from a single bolt
Of blue; but the bay is quickened with white caps,
Sparked with motion under the spur of wind.
So brightly lift the ruffled fir, sluicing
Green waters of sound, that sun and wind
Seem mingled in one breath from body of earth.
Pebble clouds that nose up from the west,
The fish hawk, slicing air, and shadows of gulls
On new sprung grass, are fringes of a day
Blown bubble clear, reflecting time and color
Like a crystal ball—as though the world,
Created new, found bright completion here.

The Published Year: To the Children of Green Acres School

What motion's here to check the season
Still plumed with green, though frost's old lesson
Is published in the scarlet creeper
That freckles sunny walls while steeper
Shadows climb the western lawn?
Still, summer seems a landscape drawn
Forever on a leaf light sky,
And autumn stands forever in the dry
Bronze pyramid of corn,
And the pear tree, dangling fruit, yet shorn
Of leaves. Beneath it, children crown the ripe
Day with laughter. Flower-striped
With sweaters, see them reach for sheaves
Of grass, or burrow where the cornstalk weaves
Tall peaked hats with tassels on,
Above gold pumpkins, glossed with sun.

Theirs is the full, the published year.
Straight blade, round fruit and all the clear
Sharp hazard of the turning leaf
Live in firm bodies for one brief
Bright gesture on the wall of time
And trace the year's old, perfect rhyme.

Why Should We Seek to Do it All

Why should we seek to do it all?
Spring is not confused.by fall,
The oak tree never tells the beach
There's room alone for russet speech,
And no brook wonders if her springs
Are great or small—of it the ocean sings.
They know, and knowing, are content to be.
The whole wide orchestra of earth gives sound
To each who tunes his fiddle simply
On his holy ground.

Come June

Come June and all the girls and boys
Are free as robins in the bubbling air.
Come June and all the wheat is golden fleshed
And night wears fireflies in her hair.
The rose has tumbled over every fence
In privacy of bloom
And all the brooks are silver flushed
With song of knowing where and whence.
Come June we'll gather love
Like red branched berries in the grass.
We'll lie where summer's pulse
Is ripening wheat
And robins build with song and nest.

Peony for Ann Going on Sixteen

The peony buds are holding
This last unguarded hour
Before the bud unfolding
Flounces the upper air.
So soft the glow of this petal,
She's welcome anywhere;
Tumbled the garden with color
And all her shaken hair.

Crescent Moon

If all the world was gathered
In homage at my feet
I'd see her half a world away
And go my love to meet.
The new moon for her breastpin
Love's garden for her seat
All the world more blessed
Because our four hands meet.

If all the world was gathered
In homage at my feet
I would not wait but only turn
My one true love to meet.
The new moon past his shoulder
The dusk hills at his feet
All the world would rest
Where love's eyes meet.

There's a new moon low in the dusk of June
Come, my love, the promise own.
Red rose deepens, blue bell waits
Fireflies pulse and wedding gates
Swing on hinge of near and far,
A crescent moon and one bright star.

When summer's crescent moon floats
Low in a dusk lit sky
Attended by a single star,
When lilies open, three on a single stem
And the red rose and blue bell deepen in twilight glow,
When fireflies pulse in windless air of June
And love, expectant, waits in tender pause
Of an hour that needs no word,
Only this perfect balance, day in the arms of night;
Ah, then comes promise and fulfillment
Companioned as new moon in heaven

The golden singleness of star
And lilies radiance below.

Ah, then comes bridegroom and the bride
Confirming all the year,
Dipping their hands in spring or winter snow,
Seeding summer in fall's depth of sky.
And all creation sings of love whose word
Is giver, re-giving in a rhythmic flow
Speaking the oneness heart then finds,
The holy trinity of life, of love.

June in Virginia

The foam is on the elder bush,
The berry's on the vine,
The brook has plumped the hollows,
On the hills are spotted kine.

Oh, come and let your warm hair blow
Against the summer's cheek
And speak your heart from fern green eyes
For summer's never meek.

How lovely lies the leaf-thin skirt
Against your body's line.
How lightly lift the winds of joy
That blow your lips to mine.

The foam is on the elder bush,
The berry's on the vine.
Need we a bird to point the way,
Need we another sign?

Streamline, Virginia to Maine

Turn from this blood extravagance
That roots me in a spendthrift land,
And binds my heart and fills my hand
With lush and green abundance
Of honeysuckle, trumpet vine and all
The ranker excellence of summer scrolled
On air and acre and unrolled
Before devouring; for here,
New England fields march crisply under
Clouds like colored thunder
And the swift, metallic year
Speeds like an arrow to its mark,
Tipped with maple on the clear
Shaft of waters, while the train
Keeps pace with time, devouring Maine.

Early Morning, North Haven, Maine

Before the day breaks wide—
Like a white beach rose,
Gold at the heart,
Wide walls of light—
Let me finger the edge of this pointed bud:
The pale blue ruffle of hills,
And water weightless as air on the land,
Fields still quiet with dew,
Little birch chip of the morning moon,
And a single sparrow tilted upon
The telephone wire.
Before the day unfolds
Its white rose bell
Clamorous with sunny hours,
Let me be still as the untouched dew,
Tender as bluet flower
And the coral drop of strawberry seed
Staining the early grass.
Let me be still as the nesting bird
Whose eyes are filmed with dawn,
Aware of the outer husk of the world
Only as a thin white shell
That cradles a new, awakening heart.

Penobscot Bay

Let the isles bell summer sunrise
And the wild loons call each other
With a sea's contralto urging
When the morning, cobalt clear,
Wades all acres of this bay.
Let the spruce-sprung island greenness
Glad the hour of noon's high tide
Lapping on grey granite ledges
Where the trees, without a shadow,
Spire a heaven's larkspur blue.
Leave to dusk in coves of stillness
Colors gentled as the heart
Listening for the hour of love
And tide flowing round the point.

Stand of Spruce

This dark conspiracy of spruce
Drawn to the water's edge,
Protesting any sudden move
The sea might make on land—
Within my heart is homage paid
To this your stand.

You breeders of all familiar spots,
Setting old landmarks up to halt the march
Of roving tides—
Buckle your bright green daggers
To this belt of shore.

Should all the southern seas,
Glittering—with rose and coral peaks,
Come riding in,
These sands would gather them like foam,
These trees still stand unmoved,
Such dark rebuff they muster
Against a charging foe.

View of Private Beach

We were not welcome on this beach.
There wasn't any place to dress.
The bath houses were under lock and key,
The owners grouped along the shore
Like ivory figures in a game of chess.
One moved into the sea,
One checked a two-year old
When water curled around her knee.
Ownership was vested in a parasol,
Single blossom on a single stem,
Seclusion most adroitly spun
Around the bees beneath its hem.

If we should break into this paradise,
Concluding that the wave was free,
The element of slight surprise
Would be more potent than the bay's decree.

Wading in the Pool

Cool, cool,
Wading in the pool
Where the water widens out,
Opal ring and ring about.
Gold light falling in a shower,
Shadows opening like a flower,
Till the petal crisps and curls,
At the heart a strangeness whirls.
Then it seems some mocking ghoul
Grins and grins from out the pool,
Tilts the sky and plaits the trees,
Bends like weed the mirrored knees.
Widening, widening all the while,
Grin on grin of goblin guile,
Out and out and out and out
Till the shores are looped about,
Rocking with a muffled laughter,
Ring on ring of motion after,
Till the wheels of goblin mirth
Circle round the dizzy earth.

The Bay Comes Home

Slack the sails
She has finished her run,
Let them droop in the fading sun.

The bay comes home
At sunset hour,
Glutted with rose,
That perilous flower
Blooming at dusk
To fade in an hour.

Filled the coves
With store of tide,
Each secret crevice
Twice as wide.

The bay comes home
And the white gulls flock
To casual nests
On an island rock.

Slack the sails
And let her rest,
Riding the waves
Like a wild duck's breast.

When morning breaks,
Loose her tether—
Out with the tide
And any weather.

August

The day drowsed and cattle sunned their backs
In clover meadows dizzy with the heat.
Rabbits limped in drooping hedge
And birds left porticoes of woodland
For cellars where the trees
Were knotted into shadows cool and strong.
The brook seemed in her dotage,
Mumbling silly tales along the wrinkled bed.
All summer was a lizard stretched to bake,
Scarce lifting lids to keep essential watch
On traffic labelled Snake.

Our Days

Our days are summer woods
Where the shuttle wind
Weaves a solid warp
Monotonously green.
But suddenly the maple
Flaunts a scarlet tare
And hint of insurrection
Stirs the pond of air.
A little boot sets southward
Perhaps a milkweed pod
Instead of dew the ermine
On the mildest sod.
Instead of thought there's whisper
And champagne in the blood
And all the sun's bright needles
Can't darn the tattered mood.

Direction

Under the skirt of the wood
The green field falls
Silk in the sun
To the branch, to the run
Of Timothy clover and Queen Anne's Lace.
Under the bow of the sky
The loose clouds fly
Eastward toward the sun's fixed eye;
And silver bent, wind brushed,
Leaning over the east
Maples sluice the wind
In green unrest.
Under the scallop shadows
Of trees and flying cloud,
Hither and yon the tumble run
Of children sparks the day.
No sure direction theirs and yet,
Against time's shadow curtain
See the varying music motion of the children
Hurrying, scurrying, all their play
Tangent to green purpose of this day.

The Indian Pipes

Stepping a wooded bank in early dusk
Just as light tilts and leaves are fey,
I saw the ghostly crowd of Indian Pipes
Pushing their heads above the cinnamon mold.
Satin filament of stem, frail
As smoke, beside a rock white-veined with quartz
Lifted a loam of leaf ten times their weight.

How frail and yet how strong to stay a hand
Though summer etched their form with shade,
A touch would blacken alabaster bowls.
I left the ghostly tender Indian Pipes
Hoarding a secret in dark loam to push
Stem toward sun and lend their light to dusk.

Seeing these flowers my heart recalled a first
Discovery, lent by another, shared with him.
Children, we stepped from path to shade of wood
And, deep amongst the trees, he called to me,
"Come here, come see what I have found for you."
There in the bronze and emerald glow of trees
I saw the mystery of Indian Pipes—
A silver cloud yet every stem apart,
Lifting a bowl of pearl, soft waxed with light.
Suddenly we were alone, grew shy as deer
With secret of ourselves and the wild wood.
One moment we stood then laughed and ran up hill.
But memory still is hidden safe as time.

September, Maine

Now on the topmost boughs of spruce
The red cone fruitage gleams,
Cattails nod in the swamp
And the evening light in solid beams
Weighs on the shaven slopes.
Mountains lie in long blue ropes
Along a cobalt sea,
Tides are heavy with the month,
And the fisherman goes more warily.
Summer gathers her final sheaves,
Spread in the sun to dry,
And a moon blown pale as a thistle seed
Floats in the first autumnal sky.

Vermont Fall

Color stormed the hills until
Sound was silence, silence sound.
The sun a lifted gold baton
Directing solid ranks of fir
And kettle drums of copper beech
And all the varied stir
Of underbrush in cello note and cymbals crash,
The fiddling birch and maple blare
And treble tone of yellow ash.

No audience but rock and air,
And cattle grazing on the hills—
Yet still from every wind-arched leaf,
The cataract of music spills.

The Mocking Bird Sings
in the Universe Arms

The mocking bird sings in the hollow of night
Telling his love, telling his love.
All of the other birds are asleep
But the mocking bird sings in the hollow of night
Telling his love, telling his love.
He has borrowed their songs to return them again;
As the moon grows full and the trees hang still
The mocking bird buoyant and tireless with love
Sings in the mulberry tree, in the dark
And light of a moon as she grows.
Low in the boughs of the trees, not yet
She rides the heavens in circled height
But tilts like a girl who is listening still,
Half ready, half waiting while he
Sings to the night, to his mate, to her,
Full of the dark earth's glee.
Oh, the mocking bird sings in the hollow of night
Telling his love, telling his love.
Sings to the moon, to the night, to his mate
Telling her all of the songs the birds
Lent him to say the hours of dark
Are buoyant and tireless, are lovely and light
When the mocking bird sings in the universe arms
Sowing his love in the hollow night.

Autumn Frieze

Now the rank marsh goldenrod
Is brass with autumn in sheltered coves.
Lavender cast her nets on the pebble beach
And purple aster opens the bayberry hedge.
Tides are fuller, encroaching like winds that ravel
The fabric of woods. Summer's deep moorings
Loosen their hold, clouds are like boats adrift;
But fields are palettes daubed with color
Whose reds and yellows will no longer run,
Climbing toward light and drinking mist.
This is the season of going and what remains
Is color and form like a painted frieze on the day.

Dimension in Green

I had been mushroom hunting in the spongy fields
Where pastures are knotted with stumps and earth yields
Pink-gilled nurslings of rain and soil that lends
A pungent savor to growth. How it pushes and fends
For a moment of life in the porous, tumbled grass
Where frost flower stares and the painted beetles pass.
Here world went green and dimension was all ground,
Padded with tufted moss and cushions as round
As globes of dew. Ruffled palms were crisped
With silver, lichens curled and pale as moon-mist.
And under the nearby spruce, nested in moss,
The red and yellow mushrooms, lacquered with gloss
Of rain, seeded the woods with autumn stain,
The first colors of fall, sown like grain.

Then out of these fields, I suddenly came on a meadow
Curtained with spruce, and beyond, the grey sea-flow.
Islands were swollen with mist and the shuttling rain
Netted the bay with a fine-spun chain.
In the heart of the spruce a scarlet maple grew,
Roaring with red, the rioting branches drew
The solid world of green and grey to a wall
Of stiff defense. But the breach was made and the call
Of a bird unraveled the mist. My world had fled
On lifted boughs and wings above my head.

Last Signatures

These are the stiller days, poised in blue,
Delicate as fireweed, effortless as drifting gull.
Sea is a cornflower meadow, downy with light.
Earth has soaked. up summer, left her to dry,
Heaping the days in brittle piles of color.
White dust of aster curls up the road,
Goldenrod feathers the fields and purple aster
Stares from the hedge or flounces a brook.
The woods give up their last damp ounce of scent,
Pungent with bronzing fern and odor of boughs
Broken by summer trampling through the brush.

This world is a crust over months that have crumbled away,
But gardens are spending their color recklessly.
Late buds rise like bubbles to the light.
Zinnias are frozen brilliance; brittle with blooming
They crowd these final hours with ochre and maroon.
One maple has raveled the green wood front.

I sat by the sea and fingered a yellow leaf,
And suddenly summer was a great balloon
That swayed in memory and was consumed
In space—leaving only a shred of color
Where limp gold seaweed spread on the rocks.

Turbulent Day

And now the apple moon
Hangs on the stillest bough of heaven.
Bird notes fall and fade
And the pale hills to dusk are given.
The walnut spreads long fingers
Unmoving on the air.
The woods are knots of calm.
Dark coolness and the ploughed lands wear
A dusky quiet, freed of sun.
Peace, peace, the turbulent day is done.

December

Now are the forests laden with winter,
Antlers of snow toss the blue sky,
Swan wing of whiteness skims the broad meadows,
And over blue hills the arrow winds fly.

Bareness and brightness bend like a bow wing,
Poised the horizon under that arch.
Season of cold and fierce awareness—
Tall and clean as the forest birch.

Now are the cities decked with winter—
Window-blaze, laughter, and music fling
Garlands of lightness over stripped hardness
'Til cold air embers and granite rings.

Praise we the season, palm to palm meeting,
Cleansed of confusion, one moment we stand,
Fir tree and holly, hearth blaze and singing,
Unite us in clasping far hand to near hand.

Winter Withered Leaves

What wry endurance holds you still
Fluttering your withered leaves.
Whispering old secrets in the windy dark,
Gibbering to every breeze?

Long since the maple spent her gold
The white birch set her lance
Drawn from her sheath of leaves
To meet the arrogance

Of winter with her burly blast
Of north wind and the wall
Of easterlies that stitch the sky
With thread of rain and knot of hail.

Even the grey beech abdicates,
Her whittled branches click
Their smoky, leafless arms,
Grown winter wise and politic.

What wry endurance holds you now
In face of spring's descent,
When elms are strung with browning buds
And every maple rent

Along each tapering blackened bough
With wisps of coral fire
Whose fragile coals conceal
A leaf in green attire?

How gaunt your fortitude now seems,
Mere obstinate decree
The situation is not what
It was and will never be.

And yet in time you will put forth

A regiment of leaves,
Wearing ruffled banners
Saluting every breeze.

I smile to think how human
Your strict and stubborn way
And then the public banners
To cancel past delay.

Winter Garden

My garden bears no purple plume
Holding the sun like a well
Where noon lies still as a single star
Cupped in a fluted bell.

My garden drops no gypsy seeds
Under the brown tent of the earth,
Gathering sun and dew to light
Their casual fire of birth.

My garden has no scalloped paths
Where snails embroider time,
Or bees go pirating for gold,
Rocking the blossoms of the lime.

My garden is a bank of snow,
Scooped with a spade of wind
Where shadow lies as soft and blue
As clusters of lupine.

Although Unasked

It is hammer cold,
The stars drill colder light
Into the black rock of the sky.
The naked elms are plucked to bone
And on the ground spare shadows lie.
The barn is a darker clump of night;
But in the stable there is warmth and light.
From one electric bulb there flows
On tumbled hay and mottled beams,
A watery light that makes the rows
Of cattle drowsing in their stalls
Enchanted beasts, known in dream
Or set in legend, spoken, never seen.

Only the new-born calf
Is real and intimate as hand.
He couldn't wait for warmer days.
This was his hour, he learned to stand,
When other creatures shivered in some hole.
He had no time or chance to know
If there was room or even shelter from the cold.
The star that brands his knobby head
Is clear and soft and shining white;
Although, unasked, he came to birth
On this the coldest winter night.

Strange Parable

That hedges should be steepled
With purple flowers and white,
That bulbs should break their casks
And perfume stem the night,

That elms should fill tall vases
With cool and clustered bloom,
Peonies sprawl in crimson,
Flags make of sun a plume?

This seems but logic headed
Toward some more solid fact—
The boundaries of completion,
December's crystal pact.

That waves should topple shoreward
And arrows find their mark,
Cities fade and stars
Make lonelier the dark,

That youth should straddle danger
Nor measure dark crevasse,
And lips be winged with loving
Yet feel the winds that pass.

This is severe compunction,
A cosmic two and two.
The sum has never altered
Since time the answer drew.

But that from wells of plenty
A drought should parch the soul,
And from ever-bearing fields,
The mouth receive a dole.

Oh, that from body radiant

With need a blight should rise,
From eager spirit's meeting
A sword should sunder eyes—

This is a stranger parable
Than grass or lips may guess—
A circle without center,
A bridge that bears no stress.

The Question

I sit so still beside you
Fearing to break the spell,
Air alone divides us,
And air will never tell.

The clock beats down the moments
Like blades of ripened wheat,
Binds the bundles firmly—
Pointed the sheaves and neat.

O love, in what torn meadow
Shall flower and drop to seed,
This stalk of our quick planting,
This briar of our need?

Will time beat down the blossom
Under a ghostly rain
And leave no seed to nourish
The frozen ground again?

Song for the Opening Year

Between a death
And then a death,
A colored stitch in time.
Between a death
And then a death,
Such mica flakes of rime
Upon the mirror
And the breath,
Bitter as the lime.
Between a night
And then a night,
A crust upon the pond.
Between a day
And then a day,
The green fern's blackened frond.

Such little nights,
Such little days
Have knit the streaming sun—
And north and south
Is core of ice
On which the earth is spun.
Between a death
And then a death,
Is prophecy begun—
That torrid belt
Has never felt the icy current run.

Her peaks of snow
Arise where flows
The stream that will
Reflect the rose.
And looking to
Those silver heights,
The heart supports
All polar nights.

Goodnight in Snow

Goodnight, the snow drifts softly down,
Heavy with lightness, the slanting roofs of the town.
Goodnight, the elms fly upward and the spruce
Bows her green branches, makes a white, silent truce
With winter, knowing her boughs are timeless,
Proof against summer and November grimness.

Goodnight, my heart is bowed with snow
That may not melt with spring and lightly flow
Into arbutus root and wild plum flower,
And young wheat blowing toward the hand of mower.
Goodnight, I pray this grief may come to rest
Lovely as shields of snow upon the fir tree's breast.

Doctored Truth

They told me of the joys of skiing,
The ginger air, the sense of freeing
Head and limbs from inhibitions
In the city's cramped conditions.
They told me how the hills take wing,
And you yourself while pine trees sing
Hallelulahs in the blue,
And applaud whatere you do.
They said that nature looks most rare
When she puts you to a dare,
And everything they said was right.
I gulped cold air till I was tight.
I spread my wings—and so did hills—
The record's down in doctor bills.
I heard the trees sing overhead
And know the one I hit was dead.
I took the dare that nature gave
And just escaped her trump, the grave.

Experience

Remembering a poet's sigh
For wild grapes on a hill,
How sweet they were and how disposed
To tempt a hungry bill.
I opened mine one day to taste
The glossy purple pills,
And straightway turned a livid green
Around my startled gill.

Ah, well, I've seen a garbage can
Topped with an ice of snow;
But now I can serenely pass
And let the damn thing go.

Snow in March

Wordless and weightless
The white flakes fall,
Each one of millions
Each part of all.
Separate, related.
Jeweled with cold—
Then mantling the dark earth
Shaped to her mold.
Sculpturing, sculpted by
Wood, rock, and hill.
Together, earth, heaven
In motion fulfill
A wonder of whiteness
That blossoms, returns
Earth to her brightness,
Sky to her mist,
Spring to her business,
The fern's opening fist.

The Apple Tree

All winter the apple tree stood—
Limbs numb as rock, the trunk wood
Crotched with years, and the rest
Dowdy and matted like an old bird nest.

Branches gathered shadow, braided it
With wind, and boughs though knit
Together, twisted separate ways,
Splotched with sun, red winter rays.

Earth and tree were sealed as one.
But under a polished sky, the dun
Limbs gripped the winter, each
Tortured to a frozen reach;

As if what held them root and branch
Together, also made the chance
For growth and balance on the sheer
Precipice of every year.

Yet when the sap rose in the tree,
And song rose, lark and chickadee,
An avalanche of blossoms came to rest,
Weightless as sun on curled crest

Of the tree. See, now, each limb has sprung
Upward to cup the cloud, light hung.

Always Ferns

Up through the leaf mold
Fern fist, fawn gray
Curled close, high higher
Fan spread to wood's day
All through the oak wood
Deep into May.
Leaf light, cool, cool,
Rain-dipped, dew-sprung,
Hill bank marsh pool
All hold fern world.
Never a month, never a day,
Heat-crisped, frost-curled,
Rock-tipped, root-swirled,
Somehow, somewhere
Fern fronds or live core
Of green fingers in earth's lap
Busy busy busy with growing
Or waiting waiting for spring sap,
Locked bronze or brave green,
Winter quiet in earth's lap.

Come Look
—for my son, Finley

He came in from out of doors,
Something to show me:
"Come look, come look,"
Inviting me to share.
I stepped into the cold March air
Gone hoarse from shouting round the eaves.
There against the naked wall
A pale shoot thrust unguarded leaves.
The year turned over, bending down
On winter-stiffened knees
I drew the frank earth smell into my lungs
And felt his hand's moist pull.
I rose; it seemed I climbed
Up rungs of light to follow him
From bud to bud, and know
Adventure's April rim
Balanced on winter air—
Joy was the hand that held
Beginnings everywhere.

To Robert Frost

I found no trespass signs within your fields,
No boards to post and owner's wrath,
And when I stumbled on your walls,
I felt myself arrested by a friendly laugh.
And yet your woods and fields retain
Many a secret stone
I would not if I could unearth,
These being the very marrow of New England bone.

For Daddy Jim and Mother Fairley

Some hoard their wisdom
Like a mine her rubies,
And some, like bands of sowers,
Fling it on whatever ground
Lies easy to the hand.
Some cry from housetops
To the multitudes below
And fly their flags
For any vanity that blows—
North, northwest or sudden veered
To south.

Your wisdom is a spring
Under a hill grown stout
With understanding of the way
That seasons go,
The shape that trees must take
Wind-watered, and the road
That men must know
Who plant their feet on precipice
And mate with danger
For a friend or foe.

Your wisdom is a spring
Soliciting no traffic,
Save clouds that slowly sail
Through rivers, blue, seraphic—
And yet, for all who would pass by,
Parched with an alien drought,
Here fountain forth familiar streams
Of kindness and most friendly truth.

Lois

Lois was fond of gaudy flowers,
Of hardy stalks and buxom bowers.
They matched her vigorous assault on life
Who was husband of work as well as wife.

She hung her washing against the sky
As though she were hanging neighbors to dry,
And she patched a portion of her own vigor
On stringy clothes that the wind made bigger.

She could tread the hay as hard as a man
And flatten it down like a palm leaf fan.
She could dominate a strawberry patch
Till the sun gave up the uneven match.

Then straight as an ironing board she'd stand
And touch her roses with a pruning hand,
Flip off the best for a friend who'd call—
Give her the flower and a bit of the wall
Of her pride and her prowess they leaned upon—
Her words were preservative like the sun.

All winter the bulbs of her fancy grew
In patterns of rugs and the quilts she drew.
Summer paraded her dahlia show,
No inhibitions were left to grow
Rank in her heart; she brought to light
A progeny that clamored to sight,
Sturdy and boisterous as the blooms
Whose nodding tops filled all her rooms.

"Those flowers," she said, with a toss of her head,
"Will drive me right out of my kitchen and bed."
It was Lois we knew who led the parade,
Calliope voice and an arm for a spade.

Prejudice
—to the Five Races of the Family of Man

There was a stone
And it would not move.
Hammer, hammer, hammer,
And the blow was blood and tears.
So we left it under the arch of skies.
There was a way above, around, below,
When the stone no longer filled
The circle of our eyes.
Then, looking back, we saw it stand
Lonely and solid, dark blot upon the land
But luminous against the evening skies.
There was a stone,
And it belonged there.
It was part of all the way we came
And direction for the way we go.
There was a stone that simply marked
"No, no, no," until each saw above, around.
The pattern made was the way we come, we go.

The Room

There stood the sofa, elegant claws
Curled under a rose mahogany back,
And the portraits under their dim reserve of years,
Eyeing the silver service where no lack
Of industry had left one stain
To mar the mirror of the hour.
And there was the Wedgewood pitcher
And the copper bowl with the poppy flower
That Great Aunt Hildah had painted and hung
Where the light came wavering like a hand,
And there was the naked stem of the hour glass—
A slim little wasp of time on a walnut stand.
Nothing was altered, not even the sun
Painting anew the old blue Delft,
No sight or sound of the soft disorder of death
In a room that held all but the living self.

Pioneer Mother

Two stalwart sons my love has borne.
Their limbs like oaks are grown.
Their shoulders broad-as a battle axe,
Their skins as clear as honey wax.

Woodsmen born and woodsmen bred.
The antlered forest knows their tread,
The burly bear and the nimble fox,
The mink, the grouse, and the crested cocks.

Meat I have from fall to spring,
Hide of deer and wild duck wing,
Corn that's grown where logs have lain,
Plump and sweet the yellow grain.

Loud in the clearing is the lusty sound
Of the axe that brings the beech to ground.
Song of the hammer, song of the saw
Bending the forest's ancient law.

Stout as rock are the wood brown walls
Where the hill-bent fountain falls.
Bed stone for the broad hearth palm,
Rafters are stored with sweet fir balm.

Two daughters I have borne,
Flawless as twin moons.
Thighs as white as willow peeled,
Faun-eared and arrow heeled.

They know the crimson-berried bog,
The honeycomb in the fallen log.
Plover's nest and wild goose feather,
Reeds to plait as firm as leather.

They know the song the young men sing

When red sap veins the early spring.
Their hands are nimble with the flax,
While the young men bow the woods to axe.

Who has daughters, who has sons,
Four seasons like a cloak she dons.
As sun and rain and snow are fair,
Her garment beautiful to wear.
What shall she want while a son begets
Her hardy dreams and her old regrets?
What shall she lose while a daughter shares
Her homespun triumphs, her woman's cares?

Earth to earth shall turn again,
Wood to meadow and meadow to plain;
But the years run smooth as golden sap,
Fall like fruit in her waiting lap.

Far in the future the cities rise
Under the bold and treeless skies,
Rustle of corn and yellowing grain
In eyeless acres of plough worn plain.

These shall be, but I shall not see.
I am the root, my sons the tree.
Green boughs above me richly I'll sleep,
Sown with the centuries firm and deep.

The Beauty That Remains

Why should we fumble with these hills
Whose stature has already grown
In beauty past our utmost reach?
Why, like an husbandman who tills
His acres for the seed he sows,
Should we contrive in words to bring to birth,
The likeness that the mind conceives for earth?
Is not the shape sufficient to the eye?
And hill that will remain though man must die?
Or numbing comfort in the thought
Of beauty that is not distraught
As body burdened with the mind's harsh cry?

Not hills that stay but times that flow
Arrest to ponder what we know
Of loveliness and change.
We seek in periods to arrange
A still mosaic like the hills—
The mind's memorial to the eye—
And thus our partial destiny fulfill
To see and then direct before death chills
The beauty that remains though we must die.

Faith

Day turned slowly westward
Mountains throning her last strength
For Majesty's adieu;
All objects that had thrown
Sharp patterns of resistance to the sun,
Under the rising tide of dusk
Found soothing and a wholeness,
As separate grains of sand find wholeness
In the glimmering wash of sea.

All sounds became articulate as one;
Stray winds ebbing back to quiet pools,
Feathered bird note, soft aware
Of water flowing under stone,
Cricket sounding out the silence
Of a shadow deepened marsh,
And hill making sure of hill
Before the close oblivion.
All sights became a coolness of one tone;
Grey plume of willow liquid as the brook,
Dark pine woven into olive hill.

All thoughts became a firmness of one thought,
When only the heart's warm beating,
Here at the close of day,
Remembers the past as tomorrow
In an infinite calm of time;
Only the spirit throbbing
Low in the throat of dusk
Follows the fireflies glinting
In the golden pallor of wheat,
Feeling the touch of a loved hand
The spoken look and the deed
Knows that all dreams are waking
Here at the close of day;
Knows that the stars, in remembering,

Are near as the fallen dew,
Whispers, ''Faith is but lengthened shadow
Of some rapt yesterday."

Shadow and Light

Now are the years like hills
In the lap of mountains grown.
What mists, what darkness fills
The hollows separateness had sown,
Divide no more the basic bone.
Now shall we lean on time
As the hills lean on the west,
Lean on their mountain wall
Whose stature, light confessed,
Grows from the mingled hills
And vales earth shadow fills.

Lean to me, then, beloved,
My hands encompass your head.
Through us again have moved
The quick and the dead.
Dark as earth's shadow that parts
East from west,
Bright as the flame that starts
From a sun's moon-covered disc,
Our moment embraces time,
This was, is and will be:
Shadow and light now rhyme
Our sure identity.

Remember Me

And when the years have gathered us
Not even the birds remember the place;
When time alone is the burning rust
That weathers the hours we knew,
In what far meadows will our dust
Mingle again with dew?
What casual flower will part our lips
To cold green syllables of root,
The warm sweet vowels of our love
Harsh consonants of growth
And vows once riveted in blood
Pale to anemone shoots?
Ah, love, ah love, remember me
Under the moss chill stone.
When some sweet boy and girl pass by
And dip their hands in spring
Till love has made their stammering hearts
One pulse where Aprils sing.

Bodies' Touch

The night was still, remote the stars
And distant every tree or hill
Outward, beyond, like nothing worth
Except some farther space to fill.
But you were near and lips were warm
And close as breath and all our will
One surge of love that made a world
Known in its fullness, dear, complete;
Confession flowing without bounds
Yet brimmed in joy, in lips that meet.

The night was far, the winds away
No hill no tree no moon could stay
Within the circle drawn by arms
Whose speech was all, whose comfort warm
From inner fires that never knew
Time, place, or ought but love that drew
Sweet exaltation, eyes to eyes
From bodies touch in dear surprise.

The Poet

Between our lips these syllables
Are consonants of frost
Or vowels that purge with severing fire
The wound of a love that's lost.

Beneath our brows these stanzas
Are graven deep as bone
To carve the sterner skeleton
When fickle flesh is gone.

Above our heads these sentences
Are trumpet vines of joy
That climb the sunlit trellises
No winds may once destroy.

Under our tongue these rhymings
Eschew a bitter fate,
Close the gaping question
Nor ever cry, "Too late."

Between our hands these cadences
Strain to Himalayan height.
The mind must sweat to reach those snows
Above the cliffs of night.

Deem not we build our castles
On dreams that rise like foam;
Their dungeons bite deep caverns
Under the red earth loam.

Their pennants fly tomorrow,
The spread of an eagle wing,
The probing beak and the pinions
Lariate the sun's fierce ring.

The lonely eye stares upward,

Filmed with the blaze of light.
Though death may be the pinnacle,
No zone delays that flight.

Poet to Her Families

Say odd, if you will,
And pity from pride;
But call me not lonely
Nor shorten my stride.

Say fickle and constant
And hung by a hair;
But death sits by lamplight,
Or rides the wild mare.

Say hard, if you think it,
The hardness of fire
That breaks with red hammers
All rock but desire.

Say willful and wayward
And wild as a faun;
Because the wood knows me
Begrudge not my dawn.

Though far from your noonday,
And coiled like a snake,
The colors are rare
As the sting it will make.

Say bitterly hounded
By self and by song;
But taste my wild honey—
Then condemn me to wrong.

Door in Time

Nothing is mine,
Nothing remains.
Earth is a vast
Window pane
Through which we see
The earth again.

Clutch and the loot
Is splintered glass.
There's color of blood,
There's color of grass.

Nothing is mine,
Not even my sons
Under my bridge
Their river runs.

Nothing is mine,
Not even my woes
I gather the die
Another throws.

Is death alone
The little bone
That I can claim
And call my own?

If death is mine
Possession's double,
For time has blown
That empty bubble.
Then time belongs
By right to me
And this alone
Is sovereignty.

With time I can
Reverse the past,
Squander the future
Or lock it fast.
Was ever realm
So broad, so vast?

Come death the final
Door in time
No alien land
My native clime.

Afterword: Mother, the Poet

James L. Fairley

Mother had three of us underlings, a word not used pejoratively, as we were all treated equally and lovingly, but grownups seem so towering to small kids, and we were so often underfoot, looking up. I, Jimmy, as she called me, was the oldest, Finley, "Fin," was next and then, issuing forth some eight years after Finley, brother Will, tagged "Willums" for a while. She treated us all as the geniuses we weren't with the possible exception of Finley who was said to have a very high IQ. Motherhood was of the utmost importance to her, which was often reflected in her poetry. She was forever describing herself as a wife, mother, and writer in that order of importance. And for the most part she was true to her self-description; we never felt neglected, or unloved. But she was not the most organized person in the world, frequently absent minded and in need of reminders. Of course, there was no way of knowing during our childhood that there was a substantial presence there living a life that had, as we were later to know, more concerns than for just the each of us.

Most of our childhood then was concerned first and foremost with Mother as a Mother, not as a published poet—and a well-respected one during her days in Cambridge, Massachusetts, with the likes of e. e. cummings (who used to let me jump up and down on his belly when he visited our house), John Holmes, Kenneth Porter (also a historian and a very dear friend), and Jack Wheelwright, as friends. Indeed, though Robert Frost was not of that immediate circle, she once told me that upon entering a local grocery store near Harvard she espied Frost and exclaimed loudly (she could be quite exclamatory, once telling me, "Son, never be afraid to make a scene!") "Aren't you Robert Frost, the poet?" He, her story goes, fastened his steely blue eyes on her and said "Yes, and aren't you Margaret Tynes Fairley, the poet?" She had several other notable friends and admirers of her poetry from those days: Norman Cousins, a well-known journalist and peace advocate, and Pauline Frederick, a journalist and commentator who was the first woman to break into national broadcasting. If Mother could be said to have a hobby horse or two, women's issues and peace were it. I used to tease her shamelessly about "skirtian nobility" but mostly tongue in cheek, as later in life I had no difficulty respecting her views. She had become more than a Mother,

Not as welcomed for us were when she insisted on reading her poetry when company was present or in a gathering of relatives. Children are terrible peer group tyrants and any behavior outside of whatever norms we kids construed to be sacrosanct at the time was considered off key, embarrassing, and disapproved of. Different though, when she read her poetry to children, whether to us or to others, and she loved doing so, and the kids loved listening, particularly the little ones. Her extraordinary gift for rhyme and fantasy just melted them away.

As a poet, talented she was, but not so in the kitchen, where her idea of a good meal was one to get through with as rapidly and simply as possible. Macaroni and cheese was served up all too often for my taste. Still she made a decent salad and, to this day, I fix myself a large bowl of greens every evening. However, during the depression when folks knocked on the door asking to do a little something around the house for food, she without fail would provide them with a chore and afterwards serve up a substantial meal at our dining room table. I remember her telling me then how extraordinarily lucky we were to have a father who had a good job and one that paid well relative to many others.

I'd never seen the movie "Gone With the Wind" until I was well along as an adult. Though I knew that the movie was shy of certain brutal realities of the racial divide in southern life, I was completely surprised and torn up by the extent to which it reminded me of Mother even then long since gone. There was much of the southern belle about Mother. Myth or not, many of those seemingly unreal traits were alive in her.

Growing up we were made aware of the brutal realities of northern prisons for Confederate prisoners of war. Both of mother's grandfathers from Southwestern Virginia had been officers in the conflict (one, John Williamson Finley, having been among the few that fought up to and over the stone wall in Pickett's Charge at Gettysburg, and he had been imprisoned at Fort Sumter in Charleston, South Carolina.) While she sympathized with her family she became a firm supporter of the rights of blacks and indeed of the recognition of the common humanity of the races. Her native Virginia (Shenandoah Valley, Tazewell, Tinkling Springs, Staunton, Hollins) was in every other respect a source of inspiration for her, with an abiding sense of place which she turned to in her poetry.

Quite un-belle like was another side of her: the independent woman, competing with men, resentful of the secondary place of women even among intelligent and well- educated males. About such is the following illustrative story: Dad's best friend over his lifetime was Gerald Brace, then a professor of English at Boston University, and a not inconsiderable novelist who wrote *The Garretson Chronicle,* a long-ago best seller. Jerry, visiting with us once in Staunton, Virginia, and Dad decided to hike up Betsy Bell, a hill that peaks at 2,000 feet near the town, so it's quite an amble not fit for a pregnant (probably with me), delicate southern lady, they opined (she had had rheumatic fever as a child). Mother felt otherwise and after they left she proceeded to follow them, but secretly, surprising them at the top, where they were obviously discomfited by her achievement. Ladies are not supposed to behave in this masculine fashion, particularly since those two stalwarts had been so solicitous about leaving her behind.

As I grew older I began to take more note of her interests. Once sitting in a car with my Aunt, Harriet Tynes, Mother's older sister, watching her coming down a slight hill towards the car, while intently observing the trees and flowers along the way, I remarked to Harriet how wonderful it was to have such interest. Harriet agreed, saying that she had had such a bent from childhood on. My fondest memory of her is of her sitting on a large granite stone that served as a step on the way out of our Maine summer house looking across one of the great views of Penobscot Bay with the Camden Hills braced on the horizon and then jotting down the thoughts and verses it inspired.

Our Uncle Finley, her younger brother, a journalist and a marvelously funny rake of a man, was a great fan of hers, noting her early concern for the importance of race relations and the environment. Once I remember her rushing out of the house in alarm beseeching some workman not to cut down a tree that had long been there. Not things: the flowers, the trees, the hills, and the seasons were passions of hers and so often brought to another life in her poetry. Years later when I became more of an outdoors person and a dedicated hiker, I became a bird watcher and now can name hundreds of wild flowers as I walk along as well as many of the cultivars. Though I heeded her passions indifferently when I was a young swell, those passions later bore fruit.

Life became more difficult for her during and then shortly after the war. Our brother Finley died of bulbar polio contracted while at a summer camp in Vermont where we had been sent to get away from what was close to being an epidemic in the warmer parts of the country, especially near Washington, D.C. where we lived in Silver Spring, Maryland, and where she had helped start one of the early nursery schools. Then, some few years after the war, she and Dad separated and finally divorced. She never recovered from this, tormenting and justifying herself for years after the event, writing endless, highly repetitive letters to Dad, Will, and myself, no small source of anguish for us too, though unrecognized for what they truly were at the time, an endless cry for help. It had become an obsessive problem and I think interfered unconsciously with the sense of wonder that inspired her earlier poetry but which now turned quite preachy and sprawled, unlike the concise, sharp poems of her best with their sudden turns in the lines which then starkly highlighted what was being said.

We never fathomed the extent of her hurt so our advice and concern had little effect on what I now know as someone who was irreparably troubled. And continuously, until her consciousness was shut off by dementia in her late seventies, she was beset with worries about her poetry, wondering about its future as an opus, its quality, or, most of all, how and when a book could come of it. Still it meant, despite its lack of completion, some purpose and hope to her remaining years.

Fortunately, not all of those remaining years were unhappy ones. One of her great loves was Maine with the little house Dad had bought for the newly marrieds in 1929 for a mere $500, on Eagle Island. After the war it had not been used for some years and needed serious improvements, so Mother, with funds she had received from her Uncle Buford, a Huntington, West Virginia millionaire, decided suddenly that the house should be fixed. And it was. For summer after summer the two of us, and sometimes Will when school didn't intrude, would journey up to Maine and work on the house. The house, close to 175 years of age, remains as a gathering point for our family every summer, a legacy from her as important as her poetry for us. There she spent much of the time writing, a lot of it prose, but that definitely not her forte as she, not being a scholar or much of a reader, over generalized and overworked the same themes, though all of it deeply felt.

Maine too was the source of many friends, some of them summer folk like ourselves, including the painter Fairfield Porter and his poet wife Anne. Perhaps more important were the local farmer-fisher folk who loved Mother as did she in return. She had an abiding respect for everyone. These wonderfully independent souls, speaking with that unforgettable down east twang, many of whom were descendants of the old English yeomen, who frequently used "ye" instead of you when addressing others, anchored her love of Maine. She, as they would say fondly, was a "case." Many remain close friends of Will and myself to this day.

She, though not an adept at verbal humor, but never missing a beat of others, did have a whimsical streak. Walking up to the other end of the Island one day we would pass a very large, tethered ram, George. With us was an old friend of mine, Sherman Krupp, who was quite the NYC boy, a bit uncomfortable on the Island and its movie-less ways, who was prone to tease George whenever we passed the poor beast. As he edged closer to this truly large animal, Mother suddenly hollered, "Look out Sherman he's not tied," causing Sherman to lose all dignity in his rush to escape a butting that could not be, as George was still firmly tied.

Devotion to all of her family right down to second cousins and 'once removes,' standing by her children at every turn (and in my case there were some serious wobbles needing attention, and Will tells of her pulling him out of school where he had been floundering in grade 2 and hiring a tutor to help him along) were constants among her ways. Will's birthday, December 10, we might add is also the same as Emily Dickinson's, Mother's favorite poet as well as the founding of the United Nations. Mother equated this with great expectations for Will's future, seeing him as a Senator—hedging a bit on whether he might become President.

There was always, too, a touch of the mysterious in her thinking, of mystic consciousness, of the beyond. She for a time was a devotee of one Walter Russell, an architect, sculptor, and cosmogonist of some renown, and his wife, Lao, whom she visited with frequently at their renaissance palace, Swannanoa, atop the Blue Ridge mountains near Afton, Virginia, where she lived for a while. We brothers were somewhat skeptical of these nether world types but they were very supportive of Mother and her poetry.

A great source of joy for her too was my son Eliot, and the caretaking of Will's two boys, Gerard and Peter, when their family lived in Queens and later Belmont, Massachusetts. They were devoted to her, and she loved being a grandma. Their sister, Rose Margaret Fairley, is now a namesake, occasionally dashing off a poem herself as well as being intently interested in a Grandmother she was not born in time to know (and likewise her brother, Andy). Mother had a small apartment near her grandsons on Long Island in Great Neck where I visited her a few times, but by then her mind was wandering and she was having difficulty keeping track of her few possessions, including the voluminous piles of manuscripts and poetry cluttered about, which were a continuous source of anxiety for her. Once, however, we visited Teddy Roosevelt's marvelous old home, Sagamore Hill. Complete enthrallment best describes her explorations there, plus much admiring comment on the enormous beech tree, blanketed with autumnal colors, on the grounds.

And now she's gone these many years but still remains a very living part of what's still left shaking in the 87-year old me and the rest of our family. For years after her death I would from time to time hear her calling me: "Jimmy!"—a cry she would use when calling us boys in from play, an audio hallucination that I loved to hear. I count myself more than fortunate to have shared with and been a given a life by this truly remarkable woman.

Made in the USA
Columbia, SC
20 January 2018